Piano
Grade One

© International Music Publications Ltd
First published in 1998 by International Music Publications Ltd
International Music Publications Ltd is a Faber Music company
Bloomsbury House 74–77 Great Russell Street London WC1B 3DA
Series Editor: Mark Mumford
Cover designed by Lydia Merrills-Ashcroft
Music arranged and processed by Barnes Music Engraving Ltd
Printed in England by Caligraving Ltd
All rights reserved

ISBN10: 0-571-53047-8
EAN13: 978-0-571-53047-2

To buy Faber Music publications or to find out about the full range of titles available,
please contact your local music retailer or Faber Music sales enquiries:

Faber Music Ltd, Burnt Mill, Elizabeth Way, Harlow, CM20 2HX England
Tel: +44(0)1279 82 89 82   Fax: +44(0)1279 82 89 83
sales@fabermusic.com   fabermusic.com

Introduction

In this *More What Else Can I Play?* collection you'll find eighteen popular tunes that are both challenging and entertaining.

The pieces have been carefully selected and arranged to create ideal supplementary material for young pianists who are either working towards or have recently taken a Grade One piano examination.

As the student progresses through the volume, technical demands increase and new concepts are introduced which reflect the requirements of the major examination boards. Each piece has suggestions and guidelines on fingering, dynamics and tempo, together with technical tips and performance notes.

Pupils will experience a wide variety of music, ranging from folk and classical through to showtunes and popular songs, leading to a greater awareness of musical styles.

Whether it's for light relief from examination preparation, or to reinforce the understanding of new concepts, this collection will interest and encourage all young piano players.

Kumbaya

Traditional

A popular song, the easily remembered words Kumbaya translate to 'come by here'. Recorded by various groups in the sixties, such as the Seekers and the Spinners, the song reached number 39 in the charts in 1969 recorded by the Sandpipers, who were most successful with their recording of 'Guantanamera'.

Here is a good opportunity to make the distinction between regular quavers and dotted rhythms. Try clapping the rhythm of the first phrase and imagine each crotchet beat is divided into four semiquavers; a regular quaver pair counts as 'one two – three four', while a dotted quaver and semiquaver counts 'one two three – four'. The tune appears twice, the second time with altered harmony. Make sure the left hand part is played softly, in support of the melody, especially as you get quieter, towards the end.

The hippopotamus song

Words by Michael Flanders, Music by Donald Swann

Flanders and Swann usually wrote their songs at the piano and tested the results on friends, relatives and even passing window cleaners. The chorus of this song, also known as 'Mud, Glorious Mud', includes the words 'Nothing quite like it for cooling the blood!'. Translations have been made into French, German, Russian, Tongan, Indonesian, Icelandic and Welsh.

This tune might look rather long but you should find, in playing the piece, that as well as having humour it moves you along. Notice that the metronome mark suggests a one-in-a-bar rhythm, with the 'click' being on the first beat of the bar. You can add a comic touch to the bass line at bars 7 and 8, those *tenuto* markings suggest the heaviness of the hippo. There's a chance to create a mood change in the section starting at bar 16.

Saint Anthony chorale

Joseph Haydn

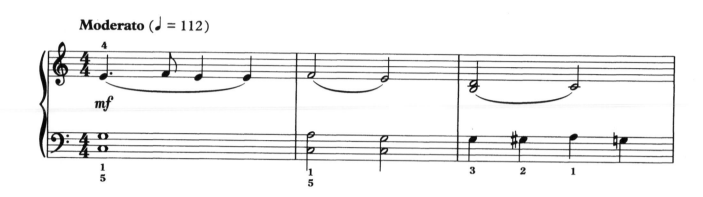

The Saint Anthony Chorale is taken from a partita that Franz Joseph Haydn (1732–1809) wrote for a group of wind instruments. Johannes Brahms (1833–1897) also used the theme to create two groups of variations, one arranged for orchestra and another for two pianos.

The main melody in this piece uses only five notes. It lies under the hand and is actually quite a useful exercise for strengthening the fourth finger. In fact, there's only one slight shift of right hand position required, which comes in the middle section. Notice how the left hand takes over the melody, in a rising sequence starting at bar 11. Be sure to give this passage a gentle *crescendo*, as marked.

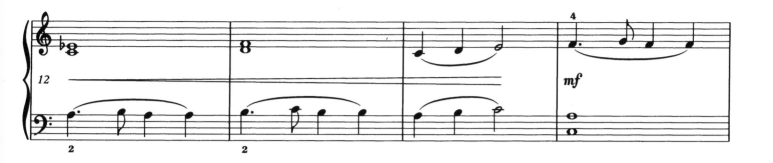

Caribbean blue

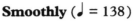

Words by Roma Ryan, Music by Enya and Nicky Ryan

'Caribbean Blue' comes from the album *Shepherd Moons* (1991) by the singer and songwriter Enya, who was born in Donegal, Ireland. Her musical style of composing and singing is very distinctive with its flowing music and almost trance-like vocals.

There's quite a lot going on here and it might be worth spending some time learning the left hand part separately to begin with. The melody is very pretty but it is really the accompaniment which colours the mood of the piece. Give plenty of thought to the position of your hands and the changes of position which will give you best control. In the phrase starting at bar 8, for instance, you might move your right hand in, toward the black keys.

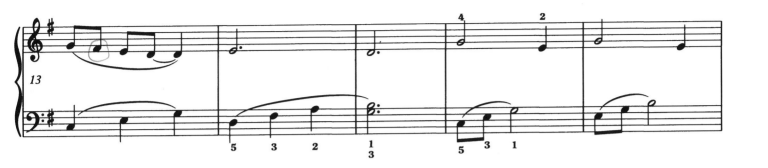

New World symphony
(Theme from 2nd movement)

Antonin Dvořák

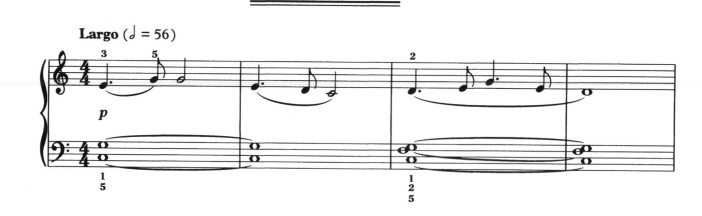

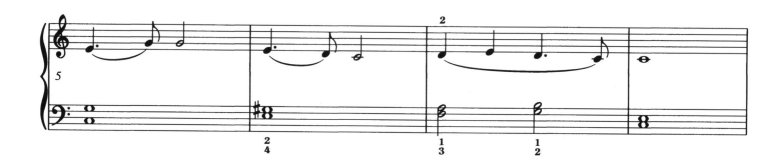

This theme is taken form the second movement of Dvořák's (1841–1904) *Symphony Number 9* in E minor. The Czechoslovakian composer spent some time living and working in the USA, during which he wrote the symphony in 1893. The son of a village butcher, Dvořák was awarded with many honours during his lifetime, including being made an Honorary Doctor of Music by Cambridge University in 1891.

Largo means slow and broad. Here it is important to be able to play gently without sounding weak. The tune begins quietly, marked **p** for piano and becomes softer still, where it is marked **pp**, at bar 13. The overall mood is a rather reflective one but there's an interesting contrast made by the left hand when it joins the rhythm of the melody, at bar 8.

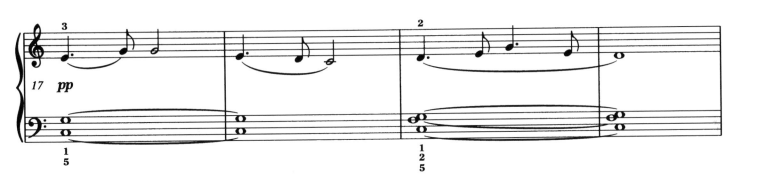

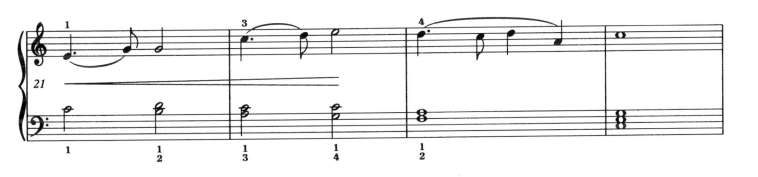

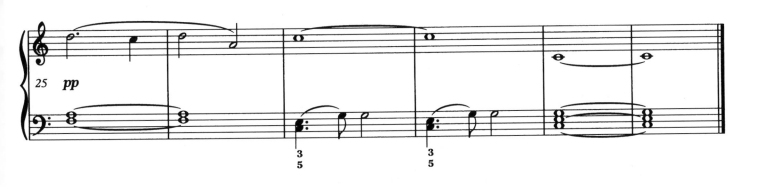

I've got no strings

Words by Ned Washington, Music by Leigh Harline

This happy-go-lucky song is from the Walt Disney file *Pinocchio* (1940). Another song from the film was Jiminy Cricket's great hit 'When You Wish Upon A Star', which won the composers an Academy Award.

In this tune imagine the puppet Pinocchio celebrating his freedom from strings. Use a light *staccato* touch to help create a cheerful mood and to suggest that some of his movements are still a little jumpy! The rests in the left hand will help you achieve this. Look at the way dots are being used, in the first few bars. You must be careful to distinguish staccato dots, positioned above or below notes, from dots which appear just after a note, alongside it, indicating a longer rhythmic value. Remember that an accidental, like the sharp sign in bar 10, stays in effect for the whole bar.

O' sole mio

Traditional

With feeling ($\downarrow$ = 126)

This Italian aria dates from 1899 and is a popular showpiece for operatic tenors. The tune has been hijacked on more than one occasion; Aaron Schoeder and Wally Gold created 'It's Now Or Never', which was a number one hit in the UK for Elvis Presley in 1960. Later still, a memorable version of the operatic original was used for an ice-cream commercial on television.

Practise the rhythm of the left hand part and notice how it moves against the rhythm of the right hand. The pause sign, or *fermata*, means you can suspend the beat temporarily, with dramatic effect.

Match of the day

Rhet Stoller

This is the theme tune to the BBC's long-running football programme of the same name. Football has featured many times in song recordings over recent years, with at least fourteen clubs having had a total of over thirty chart hits. There have also been two number one hits by England Squads.

Most people will recognize this tune in the first four notes! The melody has quite a punchy rhythm and the whole piece should sound brisk and purposeful. Make sure you can keep the pace and don't stumble over the ties, at bars 13 and 15.

True love

Words and Music by Cole Porter

Moderate Waltz ($\quad$ = 104)

A beautiful song written for the film *High Society* (1956) where it was performed in duet by Bing Crosby and Grace Kelly. Cole Porter died in 1964 but is still regarded as one of this century's greatest songwriters, having provided numerous classics, among them 'Let's Do It', 'Night And Day', 'Begin The Beguine' and 'Every Time We Say Goodbye'.

This is a tender ballad which is best played smoothly and evenly, with a gentle waltzing lilt. Look ahead and prepare for all the accidentals; sharps, flats and naturals. Particularly watch out for the A sharp, in the left hand. It's the same note as you would play for a B flat, but it is written as A sharp in this harmonic context.

Cockles and mussels

Traditional

This traditional Irish song is also sometimes called 'Molly Malone', of whom the song is about. The song tells of how Molly sold cockles and mussels through the streets of Dublin until she died of a fever – then her ghost carried on. No one seems to know the origins of the song.

The rhythm in this tune is very important. Look at the first six notes of the melody and how it jumps off the down beat of the second bar. That really is the essential building block for the whole piece. It has the characteristic 'snap' of a folk song but here needs to be kept fairly light.

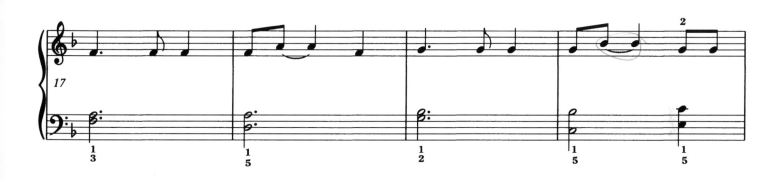

Cwm Rhondda

Geiriau Cymraeg gan Ann Griffiths, English words by Peter Williams and William Williams, Music traditional

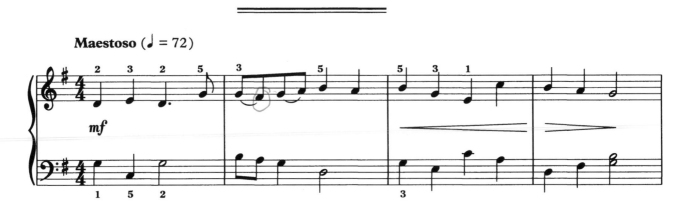

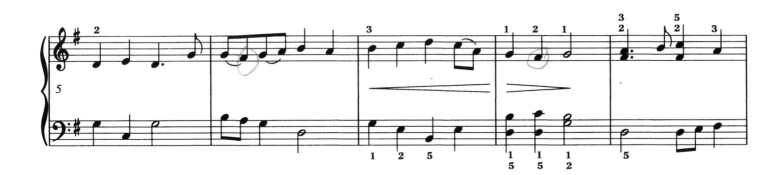

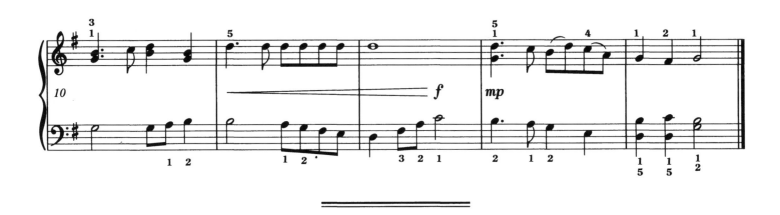

Cwm Rhondda is one of Wales' most well-known hymns and often associated with St David's day, which is celebrated on March 1st. The song is also frequently heard sung when the Welsh rugby team host international matches.

This stirring tune should sound very positive, proud and majestic. It will help to keep things flowing steadily if you give some thought to preparing your hand position. At the end of bar one, for instance, you play G with the fifth finger and immediately move your hand up, to play it again with the third finger. There's a dramatic contrast in dynamics at bars 12 and 13.

Monday
(from 'Seven days a week')

Richard Rodney Bennett

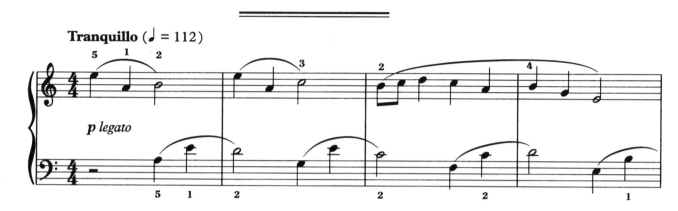

This piece is taken from a collection called 'Seven Days A Week', composed by Richard Rodney Bennett in 1962. Born in 1936, Bennett, whose mother was a pupil of Holst, studied at the Royal Academy of Music. Amongst his other published works are piano concertos, operas, string quartets and film music.

This beautiful little piece is quiet, smooth and tranquil. Notice how the melody's opening figure is reflected in the left hand. The final phrase might look irregular, as if it has an extra bar compared to the others, but this just helps the piece to reach a conclusion.

Words

Words and Music by Barry, Robin and Maurice Gibb

Words was written and originally performed by the Bee Gees – the UK vocal trio who emigrated to Australia. It reached the UK top ten in 1968 and is one of the most recorded of all the Bee Gees' songs. It was re-recorded in 1996 by the Irish boy band Boyzone and became a number one hit for the group in the UK.

This is a drifting, dreamy piece. Picture in your mind the warm, watery scene and try to evoke something of this in the sounds as they flow. Look at the **poco rit.** at bar 28.

Postman Pat

Words and Music by Bryan Daly

Postman Pat and his black and white cat called Jess first appeared on our TV screens in 1982. The characters and the theme music have since been seen and heard all over the world. The song was recently performed in Norway by the Bergen Philharmonic Orchestra and sung entirely in Norwegian!

This should be light and cheerful. Don't be alarmed by the change of time signature in the first line, it's just the way Pat himself hums it! You can play straight through, if in doubt count in crotchets, there shouldn't be any sense of interruption. As always, look out for the accidentals and don't forget to chuckle after the pause at bar 30!

The alley cat song

Words by Jack Harlen, Music by Frank Bjorn

Moderately (♩ = 108)

This song has been recorded by various artists including Peggy Lee, who also wrote the song 'He's a Tramp' and was the voice of the characters Peg and the Siamese Cats in the Walt Disney animated classic *Lady and the Tramp* (1955).

This is fun to play but it's definitely another case of having a careful look at the fingering first and knowing which way the accidentals want you to shift. After some practise you should really be able to enjoy playing the melody against the 'pad pad' of the bass line and building up the drama of the dynamic contrasts in bars 16 to 24.

© 1961 & 1998 Eureka Anstalt

Warner/Chappell Music Ltd, London W1Y 3FA

Have yourself a merry little Christmas

Words and Music by Hugh Martin and Ralph Blane

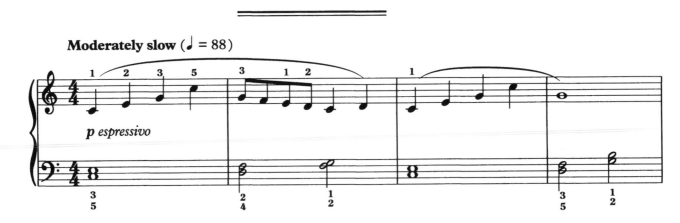

A real perennial Christmas favourite by Hollywood song writing partners Ralph Blane and Hugh Martin, this song has been recorded by numerous performers including The Carpenters, Bing Crosby, Doris Day, The Jackson Five, Barry Manilow, Frank Sinatra and Barbra Streisand.

There's a lot to watch out for here, on top of which, you're expected to play with feeling! Have a careful look at the left hand part, there are accidentals to remember and, at bars 17 to 19, some chords written up in the treble clef. As soon as you're getting to grips with the notes of each four bar phrase begin to think about how the dynamics marked will help to shape the phrase and make it sound that much richer.

(Meet) The Flintstones

Words and Music by William Hanna, Joseph Barbera and Hoyt Curtin

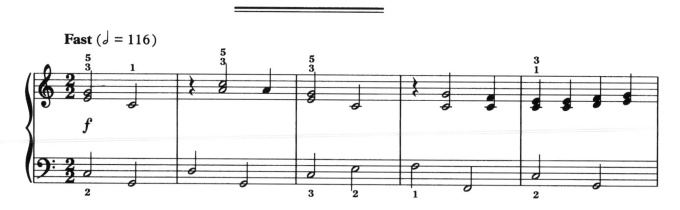

This is the theme tune to the popular animated cartoon series written by William Hanna, Joseph Barbera and Hoyt Curtin. The song was recorded by the American group the BC-52's to accompany the 1994 film, and became a top ten hit in the UK.

Eventually your performance should have plenty of enthusiasm and 'Yabba dabba doo' but choose a slow and steady pace to begin with, you need to develop precision before speed! Look carefully at the fingering in the right hand. The main tune is there at the top and the other notes add close harmonies, which make it sound brighter.

We have all the time in the world

Words by Hal David, Music by John Barry

This was the theme song of the 1969 James Bond film *On Her Majesty's Secret Service*, sung by Louis Armstrong. Although this piece of music doesn't reflect it, the film was full of nail-biting excitement. George Lazenby replaced Sean Connery as James Bond, and the film also starred Diana Rigg and Telly Savalas.

Practise the rhythms in this piece, you can do this just by tapping. There are a lot of dotted notes here, particularly the pattern in the left hand, and in most bars the hands are moving at different times. Notice how, toward the end, that pattern appears in the upper part as well.